Claretians in America

a pictorial history: 1902-2012

Malachy R. McCarthy

Daniel E. Magner, CMF

Claretian Missionaries — USA-Canada Province

St. Anthony Mary Claret, Founder
1807–1870

Claretians in America: A Pictorial History 1902–2012

© 2015 Claretian Missionaries — U.S.A.

10 9 8 7 6 5 4 3 2

Claretian Missionaries — USA-Canada Province
205 West Monroe Street, 5th floor
Chicago, Illinois 60606
312-544-8163

ISBN 978-0-89570-002-5

usaprovince@claretians.org
www.claretiansusa.org

Table of Contents

Message from the Provincial Superior
Rev. Rosendo Urrabazo, CMF

Documenting the history of the Claretians in the United States is no small matter. Our Congregation was founded by St. Anthony Mary Claret in Vic, Spain, in 1849. By the beginning of the 20th century the congregation of missionaries were over a thousand members with communities all over Spain, Africa, and Latin America. They came to the United States from Mexico at the invitation of a Texas bishop and from there spread west and north, always responding to the growing needs of Spanish-speaking Catholics.

The ministry of the Claretians has extended to immigrant communities across the country as well as to many forms of evangelization and pastoral work among youth, families, and other immigrant communities. Working with many lay collaborators, our missionaries are also involved in works of charity, seminary teaching, retreats, mission preaching, and hospital and university chaplaincies.

From the U.S., American missionaries have been sent to begin missions in Central America, Africa, the Philippines, and Europe. Their stories and the heroic efforts of so many missionaries who left family and country to witness to the gospel here and around the world remains to be told.

This book is but a small glimpse at some of the moments of the last hundred or so years. My hope is that more historical work will be forthcoming. Our men deserve to be remembered and celebrated for the good work they have done with the people they served. Their lives are an inspiration of selfless dedication to the people they serve and the church they love. Let us pray for them and for God's call to more young men and women with the same heart and generous spirit.

Thank you to our archivist Dr. Malachy McCarthy and Bro. Dan Magner, CMF, who have worked tirelessly to bring this project to completion. Thank you also to all our supportive staff at the St. Jude League, especially Ms. Carrie Bruggers, who have used their editorial and production skills to make this pictorial history of the Claretians a reality.

Introduction

The Missionary Sons of the Immaculate Heart of Mary, better known as the Claretians, entered into the United States primarily to serve the Mexican Catholic community. Unlike similar ethnic religious congregations who arrived in the U.S., the Claretians' mission faced a series of adversities that made their ministry challenging.

Different from other ethnic groups, the U.S. Mexicans they served were not immigrants but had resided in the territory for generations. The creation of the Texas Republic in 1836 altered the Mexican resident status, which became permanent after the Mexican-American War of 1846–1848. With the annexation of Mexican lands by the United States, Mexicans experienced the border that separated them from their homeland. With Spanish as their primary language, the Mexican social status lessened as Anglo-American residents inundated the region. Along with the English language came an aggressive and well-funded Protestant proselytization program whose goal was to convert the Mexican Catholic population to evangelical beliefs. Texas became the first battleground in this intra-religious conflict.

With the transformation of the former Mexican territory as part of the U.S., new Roman Catholic bishops were appointed. Finding their vicariates and dioceses decimated by the loss of Mexican clergy who had returned home, the church needed to find capable religious congregations to fill the vacuum. The Claretian arrival in Texas in 1902 began a new missionary journey for the Congregation. Establishing its motherhouse in San Antonio, the Claretians quickly staffed missions in Texas, Arizona, California, and Kansas.

With limited funds and great distances between assignments, the Claretians followed in the steps of their founder, St. Anthony Mary Claret. Hardships were to be expected, but the commitment to preach the gospel and provide the sacraments was paramount. Their ministry became problematic as they had to contend with the turmoil resulting from the Mexican Revolution; this turmoil lasted from 1910 to about 1930. The Revolution forcibly removed the role of the Catholic Church in society, resulting in the Mexican Claretians seeking refuge in the U.S. from 1914 to 1918 and 1926 to 1930—including an increased movement of Mexicans north. Few U.S. ethnic religious congregations faced the adversities the Claretians experienced. Faithful to their missionary vocation, they weathered the storm.

Building on this substantive beginning, the Claretian story provides a unique perspective in the life of the Catholic Church in the United States. *Claretians in America: A Pictorial History 1902-2012* offers a glimpse of history. Divided into four chapters, the book describes the transitions in the United States Claretian mission. The Pioneer Years chapter relates the difficulties initially faced by the community that was torn between the Anglo-American authoritative presence in the U.S. and the political turmoil in Mexico. The second chapter, focusing on Consolidation, reflects how the Congregation responded to the needs of the United States episcopate who sought out the Claretians to provide Spanish-speaking ministry. A hallmark of the missionaries was that the local community lived in the same neighborhoods as their parishioners and ministered to the peoples' needs around the clock. The Winds of Change chapter highlights the impact of the Second Vatican Council on the Claretian charism. Returning to the roots of St. Anthony Mary Claret, the United States Claretians embraced a global missionary outreach and provided social services to the poor whom they lived among. Finally, the chapter Envisioning the Future describes how the Claretian mission is experienced today. Still responsive to the needs of the local community, the Congregation developed new ministries and programs to fulfill their missionary vocation.

Unfortunately not every ministry could be represented in this book, but it is hoped that this work will provide a new understanding of the U.S. Claretian experience and inspire individuals to learn more about its history and be concerned about documenting current activities for future members and associates.

Pioneer Years
1902–1922

The Claretians entered the United States in 1902 under the sponsorship of the Mexican Province. Invited by Peter Verdaguer, Apostolic Vicar of Brownsville, Texas, their initial task was preaching missions to the Spanish-speaking people of Texas. These were years of arduous catechetical work and hardship.

At the turn of the century, the borders between Mexico and the United States were open and residents had minimal restrictions when it came to travel. Consequently, many Mexicans came to the United States to earn money and then would return to their homes in Mexico. The 1910 Mexican Revolution impacted daily life in Mexico, and many Mexican Catholics moved to the United States to escape the civil war that took on a decidedly anti-religious tone.

In response to this international situation, the Claretians opened new ministries to handle the burgeoning immigrant population. They also offered hospitality to the exiled Mexican episcopacy and Claretians who fled their homes to seek safety from persecution.

Like St. Anthony Mary Claret, the United States Claretians encountered adversity and civil strife while building a foundation for their United States enterprise.

Peter Verdaguer, Vicar Apostolic of Brownsville, Texas, 1890–1911

Bishop Verdaguer was a Catalan who left Spain and was ordained a priest to work in the United States. Fr. Verdaguer served at Our Lady Queen of Angels in Los Angeles and San Gabriel mission. Appointed Apostolic Vicar in 1890, he renewed his ties to the Claretians, having personally known the founder and his successor, Fr. Xifré. When the opportunity presented itself, he invited the Claretians to Texas to minister to the Spanish-speaking population of the state. This relationship resulted in invitations from other Western dioceses to open Claretian missions in their regions.

First Claretian Community, 1902

John Anthony Forest, Bishop of San Antonio, invited the Claretians to assume the ministry at San Fernando Cathedral. Pictured here are the first Claretians: *(L to R)* Frs. Camilo Torres, Ramón Prat, Provincial, Bishop Forest, Frs. Bernabé Marinas, Local Superior, and León Monasterio.

San Antonio Main Plaza, 1902

The Claretians entered San Antonio, Texas' largest city and the center for the Roman Catholic Church in the Lone Star State. With a population of just over 53,000 people, the city welcomed many Mexican nationals who had easy access to the United States at the turn of the century. In the city's main plaza, the government and ecclesiastical structures reflected the Spanish urban planning. Built in 1869, San Fernando Cathedral maintained a prominent place in this space.

Texas Mission Church

Local Mexicans flocked to mission churches, where the Claretians provided catechetical instruction and the sacraments. Many of these churches were built with Catholic Extension Society funding.

Texas Christmas Celebration

Flags of the United States and Mexico are used to herald the symbolic arrival of the Virgin.

Southern Messenger, February 19, 1903

The state-wide Catholic diocesan newspaper highlighted Fr. Camilo Torrente's missions in northern Texas. The local Catholic community welcomed the Claretians and their work with the Mexican Catholic community.

SOUTHERN MESSENGER.

PUBLISHED WITH THE APPROBATION OF Rt. Rev. J. A. FOREST, D.D., BISHOP OF SAN ANTONIO, AND OF Rt. Rev. PETER VERDAGUER, D. D., VICAR APOSTOLIC OF BROWNSVILLE.

VOL. XI—No. 52.]   SAN ANTONIO, TEXAS, THURSDAY, FEBRUARY 19, 1903   [PRICE $1.50 A YEAR

MISSIONS TO THE MEXICANS.

During the month of January just past Rev. Camillo Torrente of San Fernando Cathedral, San Antonio, gave a week's mission to the Mexican Catholics at each of the following places: Weatherford, Bridgeport, and Thurber, all in the diocese of Dallas.

Commencing on the feast of the Annunciation, March 25, the same Rev. Father will give a week's mission to the Mexicans of Bandera and vicinity.

The Catholic Democratic League, recently organized in England already has secured 8,000 signatures in London and Liverpool.

The Mexican-United States Province

The Province petitioned the General Government in Rome to be able to serve in local parishes. According to Claretian practices, priests always served as missioners on the road. The permission to diverge from custom allowed the Claretians to build a strong local foundation centered around parish life. From this base other missionary endeavors began.

Foundation House, San Antonio, Texas, 1903

The completion of the foundation house in San Antonio provided a new base of operations for the Claretian mission. Located conveniently near the train station and San Fernando Cathedral, the residence welcomed Claretians and other religious, clergy and bishops who sought refuge during the Mexican Revolution. This 1911 photo captures Bishop John Shaw's visit with his Claretian colleagues who administered the cathedral.

San Marcos, Texas.

St. John the Evangelist Church, San Marcos, Texas

The first permanent mission outside San Antonio began in 1905, when Fr. Eugene Sugranes traveled to San Marcos to minister to the local community. Within a year, a parish house was established with a resident community serving the parish. San Marcos presented a unique challenge, since the Protestants made life difficult for the developing community. In 1915, the parish house was destroyed by fire. A new church and rectory were constructed and dedicated to St. John the Evangelist. The parish boundaries covered 2,500 miles.

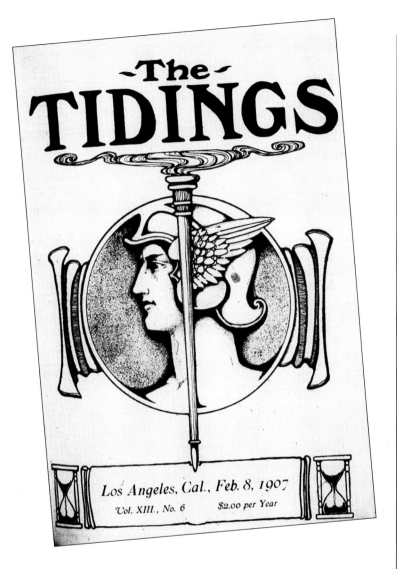

Announcement by Bishop Conaty, Claretian Jurisdiction over Mexican Catholics in Los Angeles, February 8, 1907

Bishop Conaty declared that the Claretians would exclusively serve the Spanish-speaking population of his diocese, and this prototype was used by other bishops when welcoming the Claretians to their dioceses. Initially the Claretians settled at the San Fernando Mission but within a year requested to be moved to San Gabriel Mission.

SAN FERNANDO MISSION.

Community of Priests Having Special Care of Mexican Missions Will Locate at Historic Point.

The following announcement is one of the most important which Bishop Conaty has made for some time. It means the coming to the Diocese of a new community of Priests who will have the special care of missions among the Mexicans. This religious community is of Spanish foundation and is known as "The Sons of the Immaculate Heart of Mary" and will locate in the Parish of San Fernando, over which they will have parochial rights. The Provincial Superior, Very Rev. Father Prat, C. M. F., and the Superior of the Cathedral at San Antonio, Texas, Rev. B. Marnas, C. M. F., have been in the city the past week consulting with Bishop Conaty concerning the plans for their future work in the Diocese.

The agreement which has been approved by the Diocesan Consultors, has been signed by the Bishop and by the Superior of the community, and the Fathers will probably assume charge of San Fernando next week. Besides the parochial work at San Fernando and its missions, these Fathers will be prepared to assist the pastors of the Diocese in the spiritual work among the Mexicans or any other work to which they may be invited. It is the intention of the Superior to send three Fathers to this mission.

As soon as it is possible to arrange it, the Bishop hopes that the Fathers will have charge of the old San Fernando mission to which they look forward with great interest in the desire of its restoration. The recent talk of the Mission being an amusement center is seen to be entirely out of line with any of Bishop Conaty's thoughts, as may be seen by the present arrangement. It is his desire to have it a religious center—what it was in the olden time.

It will be interesting to know that this religious Order of priests dates its origin from about the same time as the foundation of the Sisters of the Immaculate Heart who are doing educational work in the Diocese and whose Motherhouse is at Hollywood.

The Order of the Sons of the Immaculate Heart of Mary was established in Spain in 1849 by Archbishop Anthony Claret, who has since been declared Venerable by the Church. The general Motherhouse is in Spain at Aranda de Duero, near Burgos. The Motherhouse for this continent is in the City of Mexico to which the Fathers came some twenty-three years ago. There are at present nine houses of the Order in Mexico. The first establishment in the United States was made at San Antonio, Texas, four and one-half years ago. There is a second house at San Marcos in Texas, and the San Fernando foundation will be the third establishment of the Order in the United States. Brazil, the Argentine Republic and Chili, as well as Africa, has communities of this Order. There are many houses in Spain, Portugal and one in Rome. At present there are two thousand priests and Brothers belonging to the Order the object of which is to give missions and retreats.

San Gabriel Mission

In 1908, the Claretians opened their California ministry site at San Gabriel Mission. The mission served the Catholic Church since 1771 and was the mother church of Los Angeles. Following in the footsteps of the Jesuit and Franciscan missionaries, the parish became a center for Spanish-speaking catechetical activity.

Claretian Mission, Kyle, Texas

With the San Marcos community well established, local regional missions were then created. The Kyle mission met with significant challenges—the church was destroyed four different times by tornadoes and rebuilt after each catastrophe. This photo captured one of the reconstruction efforts.

Our Lady Queen of Angels (La Placita), Los Angeles, California, 1910

The acceptance of La Placita as a Claretian parish provided the Province with a permanent presence in Los Angeles. As the oldest functioning parish in the city, it became the mother church of the local community. Centrally located in the "Old Pueblo," it is conveniently situated near the train station.

Christmas Celebration at the Plaza

Our Lady Queen of Angels Church in Los Angeles became an anchor for the local community, as evidenced by this Christmas celebration.

Immaculate Heart of Mary Church, San Antonio, Texas, 1911

The Foundation House chapel became too small to serve the needs of the neighborhood, and in 1909 the Claretians received permission to become a Spanish-speaking parish. During the next two years the community constructed an impressive church employing Mexican laborers. Designed by respected San Antonio architect, Leo M. J. Dielmann, the building became a landmark on the West Side of the city.

Dodge City Mission, Kansas, 1913–1916

The Mexican community provided fertile ground for the Claretian mission, with migrants moving throughout the United States via the railroad system. Requests for Claretian priests came from all over the United States. In 1913, a band of missioners were sent to Dodge City and opened a mission. This enterprise was short-lived because misunderstandings arose between Anglo and Mexican Catholics, which led the Claretians to withdraw from Kansas.

Poteet Church, Texas.

Poteet—Texas Mission

San Antonio offered a central location for Claretian Texas missionary activity.
Fr. James Tort is pictured with the faithful in Poteet.

Mexican Exiles in San Antonio, 1914–1921

The Mexican Revolution forced bishops, priests, and religious to move to San Antonio to escape religious persecution. The city's proximity and safe distance from the border offered the exiles safety and security. In 1914, the Mexican Claretian community relocated to the city to seek refuge. Shortly afterwards, the Claretian Superior General Martín Alsina arrived to assist the exiled Claretian community. Pictured left to right in the first row is Fr. Félix Cépeda, the Mexican Provincial, Bishop Maximino Ruíz y Flores of Chiapas, in exile, Superior General Martín Alsina, and Fr. Dominic Zaldívar with the San Antonio community.

Immaculate Conception Church, Yuma, Arizona

Border churches offered sanctuary and assistance to Mexican Catholics. In 1914, the Claretians accepted Immaculate Conception parish and assisted those escaping the Mexican turmoil. Immediately, the Claretians opened a number of mission churches to minister to the increasing number of immigrants entering the United States. Pictured here is the 1919 community under the leadership of Fr. Alfonso Pujol, who is seated on the left.

Holy Family Church, Jerome, Arizona

Bishop Henry Regis Granjon of Tucson pressed the Claretians to minister at Holy Family Church. Previously staffed by French clergy, many priests returned to France to serve their home front during the First World War. Considered an interim responsibility, the Claretians remained until 1979. As a mining town attracting international laborers, the church ministered to a variety of ethnic groups.

St. Joachim's Church and Missions, Newman, California, 1914

With the rapid growth of the West, local bishops sought out religious orders to staff the vast mission areas of their dioceses. In 1914, Archbishop Patrick Riordan invited the Claretians to take over the mission field in California's Central Valley. The new foundation at Newman stretched the linguistic abilities of the Claretians as they served English, Spanish, Portuguese, and Italian Catholics at a variety of missions. Pictured is the church at Crow's Landing, a former Adventist church bought by the Province.

Sacred Heart Church, Prescott, Arizona

Bishop Granjon again prevailed upon the Claretians to accept another parish located in Prescott. Situated in the Bradshaw Mountains, the mild climate gave the Claretians a respite from the Southwestern heat! From 1915 to 1979, Sacred Heart was a mission church dependent on Holy Family, in Jerome.

Immaculate Heart of Mary Mission, Martindale, Texas, 1916

Served by the Claretians from San Marcos, TX, Martindale became a site for future Claretian expansion. Concerned about the Catholic presence in the area, the arrival of the Claretian mission heightened Protestant bigotry. The mission was destroyed by a suspicious fire in 1916, and in its place a cement block church was built. Within a short ten years, Martindale would become the first United States residence for the Cordi-Marian sisters, who fled Mexico during the Calles persecution of Catholics.

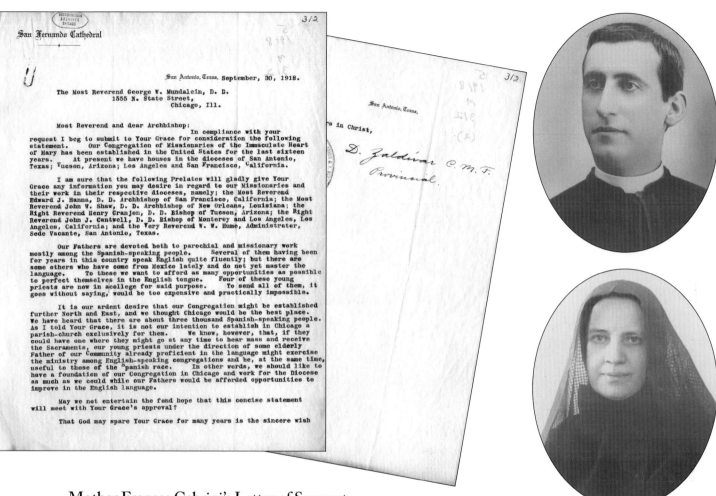

Mother Frances Cabrini's Letter of Support

Mother Frances Cabrini became associated with the Claretians at La Placita in Los Angeles. When the Claretians expressed an interest in opening a Chicago residence in 1918, the nation's future first saint encouraged them to visit and reside at Columbus Hospital in Chicago. She interceded with Archbishop George Mundelein to receive the Claretians. In requesting to establish a house of studies, it was obvious that Fr. Zaldívar was aware of the Archbishop's opposition to continue the practice of opening national or ethnic-based churches. He maintained that Chicago Catholicism should embrace a U.S. identity. The Chicago mission was postponed and did not open until six years later at Our Lady of Guadalupe Church.

Beginning of Separation between Mexico and the United States

By 1921, the Mexican/United States Province functioned within the states as the Mexican Revolution caused mayhem in Mexico City. Due to the domestic situation in Mexico, a quasi-provincial chapter decided to separate the postulancies, allowing the United States Claretians to form its candidates according to the United States experience.

The Claretian, 1922

Following in the footsteps of St. Anthony Mary Claret, the United States Claretians began their first publication, *The Claretian*. This triennial publication highlighted their current missions in the United States as well as the Congregation's missionary endeavors throughout the world. The illustrated magazine introduced the Claretian mission to an American audience.

United States Quasi-Province Council, 1918–1923

The quasi-province council directed the United States work from 1918–1923.
Fr. Dominic Zaldívar led the United States Claretians and was joined by Frs. Leo
Monasterio, Manuel Moreno, and Eugene Sugranes *(standing)* and Frs. Ramón
Prat, Zaldívar, and Dominic Carpi *(seated)*.

United States Province Consolidation

1923–1961

The Mexican Revolutionary conflict hastened the creation of a new United States Province, transforming the Claretian approach of doing mission, moving from itinerant preaching to a model using the parish church as a base for mission expansion. Ministering to a vast nation, the Catholic bishops sought out Claretians, inviting them to quickly expand in the West, then to the Midwest, and finally to the East coast. The Claretian General Government considered the new province a strong asset as they established many new mission fields. During the first decade of its existence, the United States Claretians opened missions in Panama and the United Kingdom; and in the Philippines following World War II. They also assisted the General Government in the Japanese mission.

Catholicism boomed during the 1950s as its members moved into the middle class and left the city for the suburbs. This exponential growth triggered an increased interest in religious life. Devotional practices became commonplace as the National Shrine of St. Jude and its publication, *The Voice of St. Jude*, promoted the "saint of hopeless causes," which brought donations that would support their missions both in the United States and abroad. Similar to other religious congregations, the composition of the United States Claretian province changed. The Spanish and Mexican missioners were gradually replaced by candidates from the Claretian schools, parishes, and missions. This rapid growth brought about the division of the United States into Eastern and Western Provinces in 1953. The establishment of separate provincial administrations permitted each province to respond to the needs of their particular region. The newly formed Eastern Province accepted the invitation to open a new mission in Québec.

The 1950s was a time for growth and renewal as the Claretians not only embraced a ministry in United States urban areas but also welcomed Pope John XXIII's challenge to consider Latin American missions. This era of dynamic change became a precursor of the direction of the Catholic Church at the Second Vatican Council, 1962 to 1965.

This chapter does not follow a strict chronological order but rather focuses on groupings such as Dominguez Seminary, Panama, Texas, St. Jude, and California.

Claretian House of Studies, Washington, DC, 1923

Religious formation became a priority for the newly independent province. Immediately, the Claretians purchased a property adjacent to the Catholic University of America campus, where future Claretians would pursue theological and academic training. Pictured here is the community from the 1920s joined by Superior General Martín Alsina *(front row, second from left)*.

Air Photo - Warren School of Aeronautics

Seminary and Novitiate of
The Claretian Missionaries (C.M.F.)

Dominguez Memorial
Compton, California

Dominguez Rancho and Seminary, Compton, California, 1923

The Dominguez family's generous donation of its ranch to the Claretians in 1923 allowed the Province to gain a center of operations and open a variety of formation houses on the property. Over the years, as a seminary, it has served as a residence for priests, brothers, and students. Education, counseling, and spiritual direction remain a part of the ministry of the senior Claretians residing there. Pictured here is a 1928 aerial view with the original rancho to the bottom right and the newly constructed seminary across the way.

Dominguez Seminary, 1927

The first two classes of United States scholastics pose with Manuel Milagro, Superior, and Fr. Stephen Emaldia, Prefect, seated in front of the group. Dominguez Memorial Seminary became a place where many Claretians resided at one time or another throughout the 1950s.

Wild Bill Cody Visiting Dominguez

Young high school seminarians were treated to a visit from Hollywood's own,
Wild Bill Cody.

Dominguez Family and Friends Visit

The Dominguez family maintained a close connection with the Claretians since their arrival in Los Angeles in 1910. Pictured here are members of the family and friends at the dedication of the Our Lady of Lourdes grotto at Dominguez Memorial Seminary.

Claretian Novitiate, 1931

The Dominguez Seminary housed the United States Province novitiate in 1931.
Novices Robert Alvarado, Paul Redin, John Britt, Steven Wrzyonski, John Olivia, and
Joachim López have their photo taken at the newly completed grotto on campus.

Dominguez Seminary, 1948

After World War II, Catholicism became firmly planted as a significant part of American society. Lay involvement in the church as well as an increase of religious vocations occurred. This 1948 photo captures the youth and energy of the succeeding generation of Claretians.

Dominguez Seminary Outing

The seminarians enjoyed a day away from Dominguez in this photo capturing
a break from studies during the 1950s.

Panama Mission, 1923

The Panamanian mission brought new challenges to the Claretians ministering to Kuna Indians as well as the Spanish-speaking population of the nation. The community photo dates from the 1920s.

Claretian Bishops of Panama

The Claretians were honored to have two members of the Province serve as bishops—Archbishop John Maiztegui, Vicar Apostolic of Darien and Archbishop of Panama (1932–1943) and Bishop Joseph Preciado, Vicar Apostolic of Darien (1934–1955). Both men were frequent visitors to the United States and shared their mission stories with readers of *The Voice of St. Jude*.

Our Lady of Guadalupe, South Chicago, 1924

Our Lady of Guadalupe became the Claretians' first ministry east of the Mississippi River. Initially residing in a temporary church across the street from the Chicago steel mills, the Claretians built a new church for the Mexican community in 1928.

This 1928 community is shown on the steps of the original church. *(L to R)* Frs. Joseph Puigví, Andrew Resa, Provincial, James Tort, Pastor, and Bro. James Santmiquel.

Our Lady of Guadalupe Church, Chicago, Illinois, 1928

The new church was funded by a $100,000 mortgage from the Archdiocese. Besides offering a spacious church, the Claretians included a 700-seat auditorium in the basement for social and educational functions. The new church quickly became a community anchor for the Mexican and Euro-Catholic communities.

Cornerstone Dedication of Our Lady of Guadalupe, Palm Sunday, April 1, 1928

Bishop Pascal Díaz, SJ, was the celebrant at the church's festivities. Exiled from the Mexican state of Tabasco, the Bishop would later be appointed Primate and Archbishop of Mexico City in 1929, signaling the end of the nation's church-state conflict.

The Claretians and the Mexican Cristero Revolt, 1926

The Mexican Catholic Church ended religious worship in 1926 and would not resume until 1929. The Church objected to President Elías Calles' enactment of the anti-clerical provisions of the 1917 Mexican Constitution where the Church lost its juridical status and clergy were required to register with the state to celebrate the sacraments. Because of the religious instability of Mexico, the Mexican Claretian community moved to the United States with its house of formation established on Kentucky Avenue in San Antonio. Pictured here are Mexican students with Fr. Félix Cépeda, Claretian Superior General Nicholas García, and U.S. Provincial Andrew Resa *(all seated)*.

Episcopal Exiles in San Antonio, Texas, 1926–1930

Many of the Mexican Catholic hierarchy came to the United States at the beginning of the Mexican Revolution in 1914 and then during the Cristero Revolt, 1926–1929. Chicago and Los Angeles also welcomed these émigré clergy. The Claretians actively supported the Mexican Catholic Church's position, and many Claretian priests' and brothers' families were Cristero supporters. In this photo taken at the foundation house in San Antonio, the Claretian community is joined by Veracruz Bishop Rafael Guízar y Valencia, who was canonized a saint by Pope Benedict XVI in 2006 (seated second from left).

St. Francis Mexican Mission, 1926

The demand for pastoral support of the increasing Mexican community resulted
in the Claretians accepting the formerly German parish, St. Francis of Assisi, as a
Spanish-speaking parish. In 1926, Chicago hosted a special event—the Twenty-
Eighth International Eucharistic Congress, which for the first time was held in
the United States. The Claretians were appointed to take care of the Spanish-
speaking delegates and host a meeting at St. Francis on June 20, 1926, with
Vicente Cardinal Casanova of Granada, Spain presiding. This photo captures the
close of the session.

First United States Provincial Chapter, January 1929, San Antonio, Texas

The first provincial chapter included superiors and delegates from all of the United States houses. Andrew Resa, the first United States Provincial is seated fifth from the left.

St. Jude Devotion, February 17, 1929

Our Lady of Guadalupe pastor James Tort inaugurated the national devotion to St. Jude, "the patron of hopeless cases" on February 17, 1929. This devotion would gain the Claretians international notoriety and financial support for the Chicago Mexican mission as well as for other Claretian missionary endeavors. In 1937, a direct mail campaign promoted the devotion, with millions of Catholics responding with prayer requests and support for the Province and the Congregation. Fr. Joachim DePrada placed the petitions underneath the shrine's statue of St. Jude in 1951, a practice continued to this day.

St. Jude Police League, 1932

Inaugurated on the third anniversary of the establishment of the St. Jude devotion, the St. Jude Police League was founded to offer religious support to those serving as "first responders" in Chicagoland. The Claretians created the first religious organization for the police department and inaugurated the police march, which continues to this day. The League's major goal was to construct a high school seminary, which opened in Momence, IL in 1933. Pictured here are the first Claretian graduates, Frs. Patrick McPolin and Walter Mischke of St. Jude Seminary High School on their ordination day, May 23, 1943, with the St. Jude Police League in attendance.

St. Jude Seminary, Original Building, October 1932

After much negotiation with George Cardinal Mundelein, the Claretians were given permission to build a high school seminary in Momence, IL, fifty-five miles south of Chicago. The original twelve-acre site was too small, and in 1937 a new campus was built adjacent to the Illinois Dixie Highway. Bishop John Maiztegui of Panama is pictured here with the incoming faculty and student body.

St. Jude's Seminary
Momence, Ill.

Conducted by
The Claretian Fathers

St. Jude Seminary Students, 1946

The seminary was its own formation community where students not only were educated but also lived together—caring for the buildings, grounds, and working on the farm. Pictured here is a group of seminarians in December 1946 returning from work while having fun!

St. Jude League/ Claretian Publications, 1944

The St. Jude League, established in June 1929, was responsible for promoting the St. Jude devotion and raising money to support the United States Claretian missions and General Government enterprises. In 1937 the League began a direct mail campaign in the Fall to promote the upcoming Feast of St. Jude on October 28th. This innovative program was one of the first to create a "pilgrimage by mail," where the devotee received information and was encouraged to participate in the activities of the National Shrine of St. Jude, even if they were not able to be physically present.

In 1944, to consolidate the St. Jude League, Police League, and Claretian Publications, the General Government and Samuel Cardinal Stritch approved the purchase of an office building in Chicago's West Loop at 221 West Madison Street. The initial five-story building housed not only League and Publication offices but also provided the Police League a hall where functions could be held for business and social events.

Immaculate Heart of Mary Church School, San Antonio, Texas, 1926

As a result of the Mexican Revolution, the Texas Claretians expanded their parish ministry to serve new Mexican refugees. The exiled Claretian Mexican community assisted in staffing these new parishes and missions. At Immaculate Heart of Mary Church, Archbishop Arthur Drossaerts blessed the new school on September 26, 1926.

San José Mission, Fort Worth, Texas, 1926

Bishop Joseph P. Lynch of Dallas invited the Claretians in the spring of 1926 to assist in providing pastoral care to the Mexican people residing in the diocese. The Claretians opened catechetical centers, a parish school, and health center. Pictured here are *Las Hijas de María* at the Immaculate Heart of Mary Mission with Fr. Martin Sanz. In order to better serve the local population, the Claretian missions were merged under one church, All Saints, in 1955.

Confirmation Ceremony, Hermleigh, Texas, 1928

Located 250 miles east of the Fort Worth mission, the Claretians ministered throughout the Lone Star State where travel and weather conditions did not impede their efforts to preach the Gospel and minister the Sacraments. Because of the vast territory of the diocese, the bishop's visit to local parishes was limited. Therefore the Confirmation ceremony included both Anglos and the local Mexican-American community.

Christ the King Church (Cristo Rey), San Antonio, Texas, 1932

Christ the King Parish grew from a Claretian catechetical center on San Antonio's West Side. Due to the efforts of Fr. Vicente Andrés a new church was built, followed by the opening of a parish school in 1944. The 1948 Claretian community stands before the new church: Frs. Arturo Vallvé, Raymond Catalán, Pastor, Fr. Candido Bajo, Visitor General from Rome, John O'Brien, and Angel Conangla.

St. Francis Xavier Church, El Paso, Texas, 1942

The Claretians entered the diocese of El Paso in 1932 by receiving the former Jesuit parish of Guardian Angel. In 1942 the Claretians expanded their ministry to St. Francis Xavier Parish in El Paso's "El Barrio del Diablo."

Joseph Gamm, Sweetwater, Texas, Missionary on the Move, 1946

Fr. Gamm experienced the Claretian tradition of mission work firsthand, packing up his car for his next adventure!

Immaculate Heart of Mary Church, Phoenix, Arizona

In 1925, the Claretians were invited to take over Immaculate Heart of Mary Church
in Arizona's capital city. From this parish, missions in Buckeye and Tolleson were
established.

Residence, St. Anthony Church, Phoenix, Arizona

In 1943, the Claretians began ministry at St. Anthony Church. As the photo
indicates, Phoenix reflected the frontier character of the West.

Our Lady of Solitude (Soledad), East Los Angeles, California, 1931

The Claretians expanded their mission message throughout Los Angeles. They preached missions to the Mexican community who had been forced to leave their homeland. Our Lady of Solitude became a center for Mexican Catholic refugees, which included not only laymen and women but also clergy and religious. In 1931 the Claretians began their parish service in this vibrant church. Pictured with Campeche Bishop Luis Guízar Barragán are Frs. Clement Sáenz and Manuel Almuedo.

Our Lady of Solitude School, Class of 1941

Catholic education was valued by the local Mexican community.
The Class of 1941 joined Fr. James Tort for a final photograph.

St. Peter's Italian Church, Los Angeles

A year after coming to Our Lady of Solitude, the Claretians accepted St. Peter's Italian Church in Los Angeles' "Little Italy." Fr. Basil Frison is pictured here with a First Communion class on the front steps of the church.

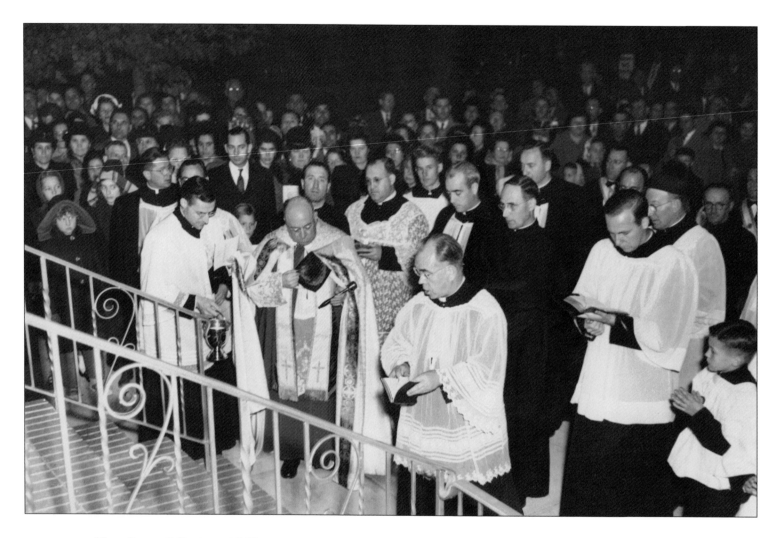

New Jersey Mission, 1948

In 1945, Fr. James Tort traveled to Trenton, NJ to preach missions to the local Latino communities. This effort led to the establishment of a short-lived Spanish-speaking mission in the city. Three years later, Tort returned to Perth Amboy, NJ to establish a permanent ministry for the Latino community. Under the patronage of Our Lady of Fatima, the parish ministers to a wide range of Catholics from Caribbean and other Latin American countries. Pictured is the dedication of the church in 1949 surrounded by the local community.

St. Anthony Claret Church, Fresno, California, 1951

The canonization of St. Anthony Mary Claret in 1950 permitted the Claretians to name a church after their founder and begin a new mission outside Los Angeles County. The new ministry focused on meeting the religious and social needs of the migrant communities who labored in the San Joaquin Valley, a major source of the United States agricultural produce. The Claretian ministry would eventually play a role in Cesar Chavez's efforts to organize the Mexican grape pickers into a union.

Birth-day and Farewell Banquet in Honor
of Fr. Raymond Catalan, C.M.F.
Aug. 13, 1948 Sta. Barbara Pang. P. I.

Midas Studio
Sta. Barbara

Philippine Mission, 1948

After the liberation of the Philippines, many religious communities entered the
Archipelago to meet the needs of the Catholic communities. Led by Fr. Raymond
Catalán, the Claretians assumed ministry at Santa Barbara Pangasinan. This
1948 gathering marks the community celebration for Fr. Catalán's birthday
and departure.

Japanese Mission, 1951

The United States Claretians accepted the General Government's invitation to assist in establishing a new mission in post-war Japan. Frs. Anthony Briskey and John Lemrise became the first United States missioners to participate. Here, Fr. Joseph Galdeano led the Japanese Catholics in prayer.

Claretian Pilgrimage to the Canonization Ceremonies

A United States Claretian pilgrimage to Europe and Rome for the ceremonies highlighted the Holy Year celebration. Pictured are Frs. Joseph Puigví and Joseph Llobet with a group of United States pilgrims.

Canonization of St. Anthony Claret

Pope Pius XII's canonization of St. Anthony Claret on May 7, 1950, marked
a milestone in Claretian history as its founder joined the pantheon of holy men
and women. The photo reflects the grandeur of the moment.

Publications

Following the example of St. Anthony Claret, his United States sons established a vibrant publications ministry. Fr. Eugene Sugranes, a Claretian editor, helped initiate this new endeavor. Three major publications formed the Claretian corpus: *La Esperanza*, a weekly Spanish-language publication and *Immaculate Heart Client*, which later became *Immaculate Heart Messenger*, and the Chicago-based *The Voice of St. Jude*. All three publications provided religious reading material for the public, and at the same time promoted the Congregation. As their readership changed, the publications integrated Catholic social action within the pages of each periodical.

FIFTH PROVINCIAL CHAPTER
Los Angeles, Calif.
APRIL, 1953

Founding of the Eastern Vice-Province

In 1953, the General Government authorized the separation of the United States into two provinces. The Eastern Vice-Province was elevated to provincial status within a year. The assignment of members of each province was determined by where they were serving so that each region would have adequate manpower. The 1953 Chapter became the last United States Claretian meeting until the reunification of the provinces in 2011. Superior General Nicholas García, pictured in the first row center, joined the unified province for its last photo opportunity.

First Postulants of Canada, 1950s

In 1953, the Eastern Province opened a mission in French-speaking Québec.
Pictured here are the first candidates: René Rivard, Fr. John Lemrise (postulant
director), Rosarie Beauchesne, and Yvon Lafontaine.

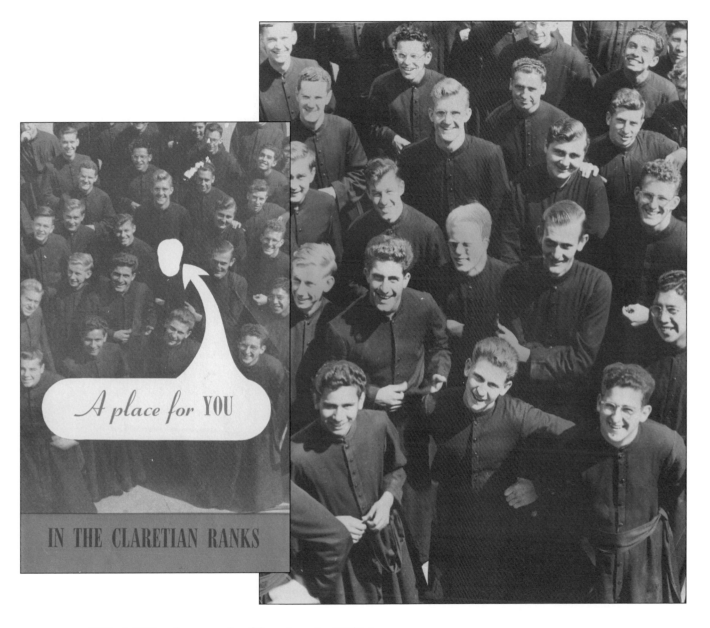

A place for YOU

IN THE CLARETIAN RANKS

Who's Who Among the Claretians in 1950s?

Did these young Claretians know that this photo would be part of an ad campaign?

Immaculate Heart Novitiate, Allendale, Indiana

Once independent, the Eastern Province had to provide new facilities to meet the
needs of the province. The provincial novitiate was established near Terre Haute, IN.
The June 27, 1954, dedication ceremony featured a Claretian choir: Richard Todd,
Orville Raeder, Tom Moran, Ted Cirone, and John Lemrise.

Del Amo Junior Seminary, 1953

The Western Province likewise needed to construct new buildings to accommodate the increase in religious vocations during the 1950s. Del Amo Junior Seminary was a resident high school located on the same property as Dominguez Memorial Seminary. Bishop Joseph Preciado is joined by Andrew Roy and Thomas Mitchell in an early class photograph.

Claretville, Calabasas, California, 1954

The former Gillette Ranch in Calabasas was purchased by the Claretians to
house a new Western School of Theology. Claretville later became home to the
Western Province novitiate. Adjacent to the Santa Monica Mountains, the site was
a welcome change from the city. In this photo Frs. Michael Cecere and Manuel
Milagro survey the new property.

Theologate, Calabasas, California

Seminarians James Maloney, Greg Kenny, Thomas Joyce, Luis Olivares, Eugene Grainer, and James Springer take a break from their studies on the grounds of the estate.

Inter-Provincial Meeting on Formation, 1957

With two novitiates, two seminary high schools, and two theologates, both
provinces cooperated in providing a unified formation program. This 1957
photograph taken at Claretville captured the meeting participants.

Winds of Change
1962–1974

During the 1950s, the United States Roman Catholic Church awaited a new vision of the Church. With many Catholics entering the middle class and moving to the suburbs, Catholics became interested in religious and political affairs and voiced their concerns. The laity assumed a greater role in the Church, actively discussing issues by means of Catholic book clubs, professional organizations, newspapers, and magazines. This quiet reformation found its triumph in the opening of the Second Vatican Council and the subsequent reforms that significantly altered the church's understanding of itself.

Religious orders were challenged to return to their roots. The Claretians studied the conciliar decrees that led to a renewal of the Congregation and its ministries. Ministry, formation, and the common life were reexamined in the light of the decrees.

Claretian Publications were impacted by the Council as some titles were no longer published, and involvement of the laity increased. In the United States, new ministries were opened, and a commitment to foreign missions reaffirmed. It was an opportunity to broaden a North American perspective to St. Anthony Mary Claret's vision of a global viewpoint.

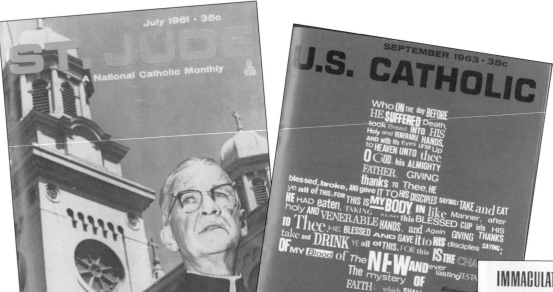

November–December 1966

St. Jude and *U.S. Catholic*

The Council's new vision impacted Claretian Publications. With the Church being viewed as the "People of God," a move to greater lay contribution within the publications was highlighted. Readers participated in periodic surveys to gauge how subscribers viewed specific issues. In 1961, the title *Voice of St. Jude* was changed to *St. Jude*. By 1963, with the Council in session, the magazine renamed itself *U.S. Catholic* to express a less devotional and more progressive vision of the magazine. *The Immaculate Heart Crusader* that began publishing in 1950 ended its publication in 1966 to conform to the new liturgical vision of the Church, which placed Marian devotion in a broader context of the Church's worship.

St. George's Church, Stockton, California

The Claretians returned to Northern California with the invitation to staff St. George's Church and St. Linus Mission in 1961. Returning after an absence of forty-seven years, the Claretians had long sought permission to reopen the Northern California mission field. Part of the agreement with the Archdiocese of San Francisco was to establish a new Junior Seminary, which would accept the increasing number of candidates seeking religious life.

Claretians at the Second Vatican Council

Cardinal Larraona Saralegui was the first Claretian member of the College of Cardinals. He was elevated in Pope John XXIII's first consistory on December 14, 1959. The Pope later appointed Cardinal Larraona Prefect of the Sacred Congregation of Rites in February 1962 in preparation for the Second Vatican Council. Fr. Basil Frison, a canonist, served as a *peritus* during the Second Vatican Council. At the close of the Council, he was appointed a Commisario for the Holy See in its work with Secular Institutes and Associations of Perfection.

In this photo taken at DePaul University in August 1952, Fr. Larraona was awarded an honorary degree for his work as Secretary of the Congregation for the Affairs of Religious. He is joined by Frs. Joachim DePrada *(second from the right)* and Basil Frison *(third from the right)*.

Mount Claret Retreat Center, Phoenix, Arizona, 1964

In the late 1950s, the Cursillo movement was introduced to the United States by two Cursillistas in Texas. Fr. Luis Dussan quickly became a leader in the movement. In Phoenix, the first Cursillo was held in 1957. Acknowledging the importance of the movement, the Claretians opened the Mount Claret Retreat Center in 1964.

Guatemala Mission

Following the advice of Pope John XXIII that North American religious sent a tenth of their members to Latin America, the Claretians began a new mission in the Izabal Department, Guatemala in 1966. Pictured is Fr. Anthony Briskey, a member of the original mission band of Claretian missionaries to Guatemala.

Mission Church, Guatemala

The Guatemala mission provided a comprehensive program for the local church. Besides ministering the sacraments and preaching, the Claretians sponsored a training program for local catechists.

Establishing the Canadian Vice-Province

In 1965, the Claretians in Canada were granted permission to become a vice-province. Besides sponsoring College Claret, they ministered to French-speaking populations in Sherbrooke, Victoriaville, and Montréal.

Louisiana State University Catholic Center, 1966

The Claretians took over the LSU Catholic Center at the state's largest campus. Ministering to some 6,500 Catholic students, the staff immediately immersed themselves in the life of the university. Fr. Joseph Peplansky interacted with students on the Baton Rouge campus.

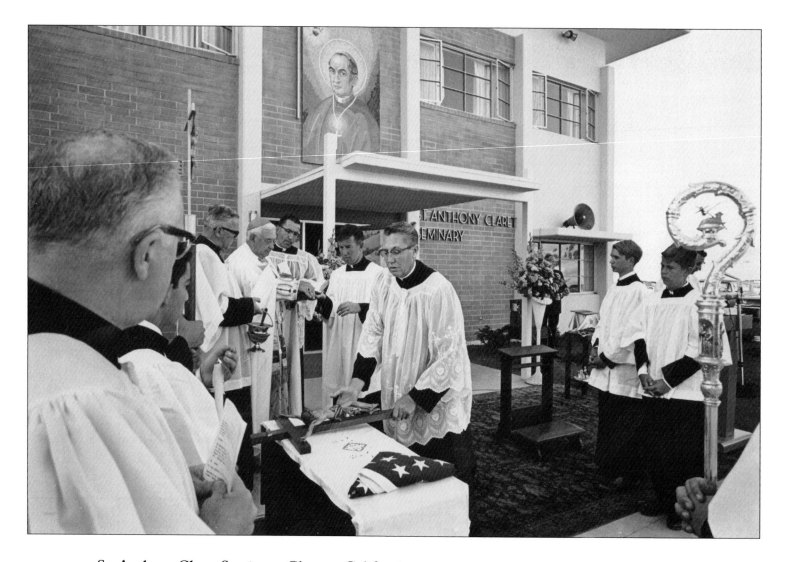

St. Anthony Claret Seminary, Clayton, California

Opening in September 1966, the new Claretian junior seminary broke with previous religious educational models as the students resided at the seminary but did their course work at De La Salle High School in neighboring Concord. Their classes were taken with local students, and seminarians were not required to wear distinctive garb. At the seminary dedication, Fr. Ernest Hyman, Rector, prepared the school's crucifix for the Bishop's blessing.

National Shrine of the Immaculate Conception Altars, Washington, DC, 1966

In crafting the National Shrine to the Immaculate Conception in Washington, DC, its sponsors wanted to have United States religious orders represented in the shrine. The Claretians funded two altars. On July 16, 1966, the altars were dedicated: one to the Immaculate Heart of Mary, patron of the Claretian Congregation, and the other to St. Anthony Mary Claret, founder of the Congregation.

**President Lyndon Baines Johnson attends Good Friday Service
at San Fernando Cathedral, San Antonio, Texas, 1966**

After extending Medicare benefits at the Victoria Plaza Golden Age Center across
from the cathedral, the president was welcomed by Fr. Peter Caballé to the Holy
Week service.

St. Louis House of Studies, 1966

After an exhaustive search by the Eastern Province
to find the best institution for their students to study
philosophy, they selected Jesuit-run St. Louis University in Missouri. On
September 7, 1966, twenty-seven students moved into the ninth floor of the
Coronado Residence Center (later renamed Lewis Memorial Residence). Additional
residents included Frs. Ted Cirone as Superior, Marty Kirk as Prefect of Students,
and Ed Andrés as Treasurer.

In 1971, the Claretian community moved into two independent adjacent
buildings behind Lewis Memorial. In 1978, the St. Louis formation program ended
as the Claretians of the Eastern Province were adapting their formation program to
new situations.

AVE Center, San Francisco, California, 1967

In a move to update the theological training of its members, the Claretians opened the Adult Vocations Educational Center (AVE Center) in 1967 and quickly immersed themselves in the life of the local community. This 1970 photo captures Joseph Marlia, John Martens, and Thomas Loftus leaving for their ministry opportunities. Later, another AVE center opened in San Antonio, TX following the same model.

Claretian Provincial Government Changes

The Second Vatican Council encouraged religious orders to experiment with changing their internal governance. Beginning in 1968, the Claretians in the United States gradually adopted the changes. Described as the First Provincial Chapter of the Eastern Province, the members not only represented local communities but also included twelve elected at-large members. The Chapter of Affairs was held at the Claretian House of Studies in Washington, DC, in August, 1968. Fr. Ted Cirone, president of the Chapter, is pictured front and center.

Western Province Eighth Provincial Chapter, 1971

The Western Province held a similar chapter and was joined by the Superior General, Anthony Leghisa. Thirty-seven members, including the elected delegates and guests, attended the meeting. For the first time, a delegate was appointed to represent the brothers.

Man Among Men — Claretian Vocation Film, 1968

To promote vocations, the Claretians made a film using the latest Hollywood-style production. Students Jim Grumish and his crew of John Zodrow and Tom Myrdahl moved from California to Chicago to manage the completion of film sequences. They shot scenes all over the Chicagoland area, St. Louis, and Baton Rouge, Louisiana, as well as Guatemala. Students undertook all camera work, editing, and post-production.

Claretian Renewal Center, Los Angeles, California, 1969

Built on the former site of the provincial residence, the Claretian Renewal Center reflected the changes highlighted by the Second Vatican Council. New provincial offices and residence included ample areas for meetings and a retreat wing that could house forty guests. Western Provincial Patrick McPolin joins the Superior General, Anthony Leghisa, in front of the newly completed building.

Assemblies, 1969

A significant innovation proposed by the Council of the Eastern Province in 1969 was the recommendation for annual assemblies of the entire Province. The first one took place during Easter week of that year. The newly formed pastoral commission would have a larger forum of discussion with the Province members in order to proceed with the pastoral planning that was given them as a mandate by the recent Chapter.

St. Mary of Sorrows Church, Fairfax Station, Virginia, 1969

With the increased number of Catholics moving into Fairfax County, Virginia, Bishop John J. Russell invited the Claretians to minister to one of the oldest Catholic churches in the state, St. Mary of Sorrows. Although not established as a parish until 1918 under the guidance of a Mexican-refugee priest, the mission served the local Catholic community from 1858. Interested in implementing the reforms of the Second Vatican Council, the Bishop encouraged a co-pastor arrangement where all three Claretians shared leadership of the parish. The community also ministered to the Catholic students at George Mason University in Fairfax. Fr. Richard Wozniak found some needed recreation as he played baseball with young parishioners. Pictured is the original white-framed clapboard church.

Closure of St. Jude Seminary, 1970

In 1970, St. Jude Seminary formally closed its doors. Citing a decline in enrollment, the costs associated with funding the program, and the need for a more integrated view of religious formation for young men, the decision to end the high school seminary program occurred. In its place, the Claretians would foster vocations among young adults living at home and attending local schools.

St. Anthony Claret Centennial Dinner, 1970

The Western Province marked the one-hundredth anniversary of St. Anthony Claret's "Birth into Heaven" with a festive celebration held at the Ambassador Hotel in Los Angeles. This fund-raising event was highlighted by the presence of Hollywood stars, Dennis Day as Master of Ceremonies, Bob Hope, Danny Thomas, Vikki Carr, and the Stepp Brothers. Bob Hope is pictured here with Fr. Patrick McPolin enjoying the evening.

Shrine of St. Anne, Arvada, Colorado, 1971

The Western Province began ministry at the Shrine of St. Anne in 1971. Informal
liturgies became a hallmark of the post-conciliar years. Fr. Ralph Berg, a member
of the parish's team ministry, celebrates Mass for a small group.

Philippine Conflict, 1972–75

The Western Province mission in southern Philippines, city of Lamitan, Basilan Island, was caught in the middle of armed conflict between the Muslims and the government. Shootings were a common element during this open war. As a consequence, there was a decrease in enrollment in the Claretian schools.

In Lamitan, the Claretian church, convent, school, clinic, and social hall bore the brunt of a surprise guerilla attack early on Easter Monday morning in 1973. The exchange of fire lasted for more than an hour. The rebels fled leaving behind Molotov bombs. The school became the home for about 700 evacuee families. By 1974, the Provincial Government wanted its missionaries to return to the United States. But the four Claretians in Lamitan—Frs. Henry Herrera and Thomas Mitchell along with Bros. Rene Lepage and José Torres— requested to remain for one more year. The conflicts had subsided, but the refugees required serious attention. Their petitions and other letters, including those from the Bishop and the Muslim Sultan of Basilan, convinced the provincial government to approve their request. The Western Province transferred the mission of Lamitan to the Philippine Province in April, 1975.

Closure of Claretville, Calabasas, California, 1972

Responding to what seemed to be a trend within the United States, large, under-utilized seminaries closed. In 1972, this fate befell Claretville, a magnificent campus set on an extensive piece of property in Malibu Canyon of the Santa Monica Mountains. Enrollment declined, and the Claretians of the Western Province reorganized their formation plans. During the last week in August, the novices moved to Dominguez Seminary near Compton, and the students moved to the former Claretian Center in Los Angeles, which became the Claretian House of Studies.

Nigerian Mission, 1973

Based on an appeal from the General Government, the Western Province
responded by sending Fr. Frank Ambrosi to be novice master. He left Los Angeles
on May 7th and traveled to Umuowa, Orlu, Nigeria, with a stopover in Rome to
talk to Father General about the future of the Claretian Foundation in Nigeria.
In subsequent years, other missionaries from the United States went to lay the
foundation for the new Claretian presence in Africa.

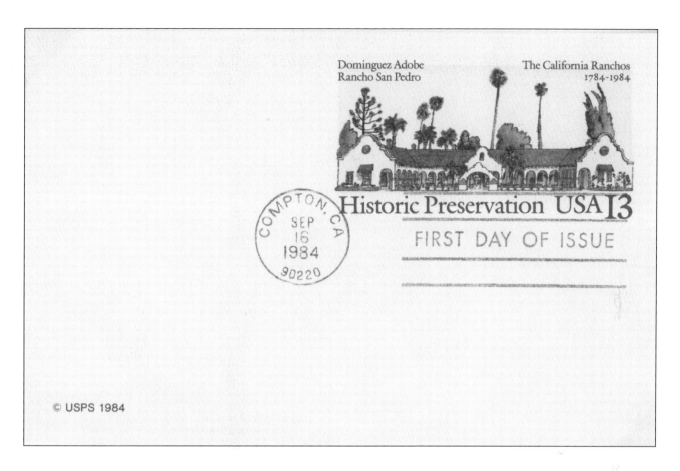

Dominguez Adobe
Rancho San Pedro

The California Ranchos
1784-1984

Historic Preservation USA 13

FIRST DAY OF ISSUE

COMPTON, CA
SEP
16
1984
90220

© USPS 1984

Restoration of the Dominguez Adobe, 1974

In 1972, after his retirement as Western Province Provincial, Fr. Patrick McPolin became the resident curator of the Dominguez Adobe. This homestead was associated with Rancho San Pedro, a 75,000 acre land grant given by the Spanish crown to Juan José Domínguez. The heirs of Manuel Domínguez donated their portion of the remaining property to the Claretians in 1923. Although a historic site in California, it remained overlooked until the 1970s. Under Fr. Pat's guidance, the building was restored in 1974 and two years later placed on the National Register of Historic Landmarks and became a California State Historic Monument. The site received national attention in 1984 when its image appeared on a series of postcards printed by the United States postal service highlighting historic preservation.

Election of James Maloney as Provincial, Eastern Province, 1974

James Maloney was elected by the perpetually-professed members of the Eastern Province gathered at the Chapter in 1974. As the first popularly-elected provincial in Claretian history, the event was groundbreaking. The photo captured the moment when the election result was announced. Fr. Jim is joined by Fr. Eugene Grainer, the outgoing provincial, and Fr. Ted Cirone, who as a member of the General Government was president of the Chapter.

Envisioning the Future
1975–2012

With the reforms of the Second Vatican Council in place, the 1970s brought a new vision to the Church. After a period of community discernment, the Claretians shaped a program that would emphasize their evangelical and missionary witness, social outreach, and commitment to the expanding Latino community that resided in urban areas.

New ministries opened to meet the challenges of the local community. The former Eastern Province made a commitment to South Chicago by funding organizations that provided affordable housing and medical care for the region. In the West, the Claretians expanded their mission to meet the demands of exponential Catholic population growth on the West Coast.

In determining a proper theological education for the seminarians, the Claretians were impacted by conciliar views and reevaluated how men were educated. With the faithful described as the "People of God," lay spiritual formation was encouraged. This new interest led the Claretians to support programs that focused on spiritual and psychological growth. This endeavor provided a means to implement church renewal as well as rediscover Claret's vision of Catholicism.

The Claretian desire to spread God's word never abated as they committed themselves to prepare members for the global missionary effort. This vision resulted in welcoming new candidates from the Americas, Asia, and Africa, creating a different dynamic in the Congregation.

Claret House, Chicago, Illinois, 1975

In 1972, the Eastern Province Claretian students began to take classes at Catholic Theological Union (CTU) in the Hyde Park neighborhood of Chicago. In 1975, the Claretians purchased and remodeled two adjacent three-story apartment buildings on Everett Avenue. One of them became Claret House for the students, which was situated only a few blocks from CTU, with easy access to Claretian parishes and ministries in the Chicago area.

The chapel is graced with wood sculptures created by the late, renowned, Claretian sculptor, Fr. Segundo Gutiérrez, whose works appear in many museums in Europe and Latin America. Pictured is a 2013 photo of the Claret House community.

Sacred Heart Church, Poplar Bluff, Missouri, 1976

The Claretians accepted a new mission in Missouri at Sacred Heart Church in Poplar Bluff. This new apostolate became the foundation of a continuing presence of Claretians in the Diocese of Springfield-Cape Giradeau. Founded as a mission church in 1876, the parish had an extensive physical plant with a large church and elementary school. The first Claretians who served in the diocese were Frs. Don Lavelle and John Lemrise.

Election of Fr. Bernard O'Connor as Provincial of the Western Province, Los Angeles, California, 1977

In 1977, the Western Province Chapter delegates met in Los Angeles and elected their provincial and council for the first time. Prior to this time, the Province leadership was appointed by the Claretian General Government in Rome. Fr. Bernard O'Connor, the appointed Provincial Superior from 1971–1977, was overwhelmingly elected. Frs. John Martens, Frank Ferrante, Ralph Berg, and Robert Villanueva served on this newly-elected council.

Claretian Medical Center Opening, Chicago, Illinois, 1978

The Claretian Medical Center, now known as the Chicago Family Health Center, opened in South Chicago to provide health care to the local community. Fr. Jim Maloney, Provincial, who previously resided at Our Lady of Guadalupe Church, oversaw this new Claretian, community-based enterprise.

St. Louise Church, Bellevue, Washington, 1976

St. John Bosco Church, Tacoma, Washington, 1981

Under the leadership of Archbishop Raymond Hunthausen, the Claretians were invited to staff two parishes in the Archdiocese of Seattle. In June 1976, they accepted the pastoral leadership of St. Louise Church. A team ministry approach was utilized and a greater involvement of parishioners in the church's life was emphasized. Five years later, St. John Bosco Church welcomed the Claretians to Tacoma.

Fr. Peter Rodríguez and Immigrant Rights, Chicago, Illinois, 1975

Fr. Peter Rodríguez at St. Francis of Assisi Church became one of the leading religious leaders focusing on Hispanic ministry in Chicago. In 1973, Frs. Peter and Sevy López challenged the passage of the Rodino Bill in the United States Congress, which radically limited Mexican admission to United States citizenship.

Quickly, Fr. Peter became a spokesperson for the Mexican community and criticized the Immigration and Naturalization Service for its policies in Chicago. The news media often sought out his opinions, and Fr. Peter was named Latin Man of the Year in 1975. He began a Spanish-language news program on the Catholic Television Network and served as director of Hispanic Ministry for the Archdiocese of Chicago. His tireless work reflected the Claretian commitment to protect the newly-arrived immigrant groups in the United States.

Claretian Associates Neighborhood Development Office (CANDO), South Chicago, Illinois, 1978

The Claretian Associates provided another opportunity for social outreach by providing homes for South Chicago's residents. Pictured is Mayor Richard M. Daley participating in the 1993 groundbreaking for the Guadalupe Homes project in the city's former steel mill district.

Claret Center, Chicago, Illinois, 1979

Fr. Marty Kirk and Sr. Mary Ellen Moore, SH, founded Claret Center to offer spiritual direction and therapy to individuals and groups. Fr. Marty Kirk wrote, "The center grew out of concern for the integration of the spiritual and psychological in the well-being of the person."

Throughout the years, the center's staff of trained spiritual directors and psychotherapists from various religious orders and lay professionals offered its services with particular attention to the holistic development of the person. Today, the original mission continues, including internship programs in counseling and spiritual direction.

Claret House, Berkeley, California, 1979

In 1979, the Western Province house of studies (AVE Center) moved across the bay to Berkeley, where many religious communities became part of the newly-formed Graduate Theological Union. Pictured here is the 1984 local community with Fr. James Griffin.

St. Bonaventure Church, Concord, California, 1980

Having previously established a minor seminary in Clayton, CA that later closed, the Claretians returned to the diocese of Oakland in 1980 to accept the pastoral ministry of St. Bonaventure Church in Concord. Within five years of their arrival, the pastoral team completed a new parish complex serving 1,300 parishioners, who played an active role in designing the new building.

Catholic Theological Union, Chicago, Illinois, 1980

The Claretians formally committed their support of Catholic Theological Union in 1980 by becoming a corporate member of the governing board. By accepting this invitation, the Congregation actively participated in the direction of the collaboratively-owned theologate. In 1993, former provincial Marty Kirk became Chair of CTU's Board of Trustees. At the time CTU served 32 religious communities with an enrollment of 360 lay and religious students.

Immaculate Heart of Mary Vicariate/
Holy Cross Church, Chicago, Illinois, 1981

The exponential growth of Chicago's Spanish-speaking population transformed some city neighborhoods. Due to the construction of the Eisenhower expressway and the University of Illinois Chicago Circle campus, the residents moved south and west. The composition of the Back of the Yards community changed. The closure of the stockyards and the arrival of new immigrant groups provided new challenges for the archdiocese.

With limited space available at the Immaculate Heart Vicariate that was established in 1945, the Claretians were invited to minister nearby at the former Lithuanian Holy Cross Church. Undertaken in 1981, the new parish, Holy Cross/IHM had the facilities to minister to the needs of the local neighborhood. Soon the church became a neighborhood anchor by providing outreach and programs for youth. The photos capture Holy Cross Church *(top left)*, a 1979 Ash Wednesday service at IHM *(top right)* and the marimba ensemble *(bottom right)*, one of the ministries that has flourished.

Sacred Heart Church, Springfield, Missouri, 1981

The Claretian Eastern Province accepted an invitation from Bishop Bernard Law in the Diocese of Springfield-Cape Girardeau to assume responsibility for Sacred Heart Church and campus ministry in Springfield. The Sacred Heart Church, built in 1884, is the oldest of the six Catholic churches in Springfield. It was designated a historic building by the city of Springfield in 1976. In 1996, Bishop John Leibrecht requested Sacred Heart to become the Welcoming Parish for new immigrants in Springfield. Today, two Sunday Masses are celebrated in Spanish.

O'Reilly Catholic Student Center, Springfield, Missouri

The Eastern Province began serving the students of Southwest Missouri State University in 1981. Eventually a two-story structure on the edge of campus was acquired in 1990 becoming the Nancy McGregor House.

Throughout the years, a variety of Claretians served as chaplains including Frs. Len Brown, Eddie DeLeon, and Tom McGann. In 1992, campus ministry also included serving Drury University and Ozark Technical College. In recent years, the state university changed its name becoming Missouri State University (MSU).

A new multimillion-dollar student center began construction in 2000, with Fr. Eddie DeLeon taking a leading role in raising funds, including substantial grants from the Province and the O'Reilly family. The Catholic Campus Ministry Center includes the 400 seat Chapel of Claretian Martyrs as well as a library, music room, meeting rooms for students and staff, a large reception hall, and ministry offices. Services include daily and Sunday Masses, religious education classes, and Catholic leadership training for the students who serve the church and the local community.

Casa Guadalupe, Hood River, Oregon, 1981

Following the original mission objective of the Claretians, the Western Province began a mission to the migrant workers of Hood River. Invited by Bishop Thomas J. Connolly of Baker, OR, the Claretians were to serve as active missioners to the 10,000 Spanish-speaking Catholics that resided in the area. A central mission house became the headquarters for the new evangelical effort. Fr. Joseph Gamm is pictured meeting with a local family in the mission territory.

Claretian Lay Volunteers, Chicago, Illinois, 1983 Claretian Lay Missionaries/ Volunteers, Los Angeles, California, 1985

The Claretian Lay Volunteer program began in 1983 to attract young adults to serve poor and disadvantaged people and to live in community with like-minded individuals for mutual support. Associated with active Claretian ministries and diocesan programs, it offered new opportunities for individuals to serve the church and local society. Pictured here is the first group of Western Province lay missionaries in 1985–1986 *(bottom right)* and the Eastern Province volunteers on retreat with John DiMucci, director in 2004 *(top left)*.

Episcopal Ordination of Fr. Placido Rodríguez, Chicago, Illinois, 1983

On October 31, 1983, Pope John Paul II announced the appointment of Fr. Placido Rodríguez as an Auxiliary Bishop of Chicago. Having been raised in St. Francis of Assisi Church in Chicago, the newly appointed bishop attended St. Jude Seminary, did his college and philosophy studies at Claretville and finished his theological graduate work at the Catholic University of America. Serving in Spanish-speaking Claretian parishes, he was acquainted with the challenges facing Hispanic Catholics. On April 5, 1994, Bishop Placido was appointed the Second Bishop of Lubbock, Texas where he serves today.

La Purísima Church, Orange, California, 1983

Answering the needs of the local dioceses, the Claretians accepted pastoral responsibility at La Purísima Church in Orange. Founded in 1924 to serve the local Spanish-speaking population, the church became an anchor for the local community. Fr. Leo Delgado welcomes and shares a meal with parishioners in this 1998 photo.

Casa Claret, Chicago, Illinois, 1985

Casa Claret was established to serve as a discernment community for the Eastern Province. This program emphasized the fostering of an individual's vocation, be it to religious life or to the lay state, by becoming more involved in the life of the church. This 2005 photo was taken with Fr. Carl Quebedeaux in Pilsen.

St. Jude League/Claretian Publications Building, 205 West Monroe Street, Chicago, Illinois, 1986

The urban redevelopment of the West Loop led to a new headquarters for the St. Jude League/Claretian Publications. Located one block south of the old 221 West Madison address, the new ten-story building was designed in 1898 by noted Chicago architects William Holabird and Martin Roche. Known as the Williams Building, the edifice served the city's wholesale district by providing space for vendors to sell goods on the business market. This photo captured the last day for Claretian employees at the former site on West Madison Street and a view of the current building on West Monroe Street.

St. Paul, Chicago, Illinois, 1987

The Claretians of the Eastern Province took over pastoral responsibilities for this predominantly Spanish-speaking parish at the request of Cardinal Joseph Bernardin. Historically, St. Paul's was considered a pillar of strength for its German immigrant parishioners when it was founded in 1876, and dedicated in 1899, but now serves an ever-expanding Mexican-American community.

The church is located in the Pilsen neighborhood in Chicago and is well-known for its majestic twin spires that can be seen for miles around. The church's cathedral-like edifice and magnificent stained glass windows are standouts in the neighborhood. The church was identified by Ripley's *Believe It or Not* as the church built without a nail—only brick and mortar. The Claretians returned administration of the parish to the Archdiocese of Chicago in 2009.

Claretian Tape Ministry, Fr. John Hampsch, 1987

Fr. John Hampsch served as a parish priest, seminary and college professor, hospital, prison, and college chaplain, and Cursillo director. Throughout his life as a Claretian, he was conscious of the importance of his preaching ministry. The Claretian Tape Ministry began when people requested audio copies of his presentations. Today the ministry includes the sale of books and a variety of media to proclaim God's Word. Fr. John Hampsch and Mrs. Sheila Evans are pictured at a convention promoting the Tape Ministry materials.

Cameroon Mission, 1987

In 1987, the Western Province sent missionaries to St. Patrick's Mission in Babanki-Tungo, Cameroon. Historically a Christian settlement established by the Mill-Hill Missionaries in 1938, the settlement was abandoned. The new Claretian missionary effort served not only Babanki-Tungo but also Batibo, where many outstations and schools were established.

Hispanic Ministry Resource Center, Chicago, Illinois, 1991

The Hispanic Ministry Resource Center demonstrates the commitment of Claretian Publications to provide new, culturally appropriate materials for the Hispanic Catholic community in the U.S. Initially sponsoring two publications—*Nuestra Parroquia* and *El Momento Católico*—the center expanded its publication base to include *¡OYE!*, a bilingual vocational and leadership development publication for Hispanic Catholics. The photo above shows our HMRC team in 2015.

Villa Guadalupe, South Chicago, Illinois, 1990

Concerned about the social conditions in South Chicago, the Claretians committed themselves to sponsor and construct a five-story residence for the elderly. No similar facilities existed in the neighborhood, where one in five senior citizens lived at or near the poverty level. Known as Villa Guadalupe, the building offers a safe and comfortable environment for seniors, directly across the street from Our Lady of Guadalupe Church.

Dominguez Seminary, Dominguez Hills, California, 1992

The plans to renovate the Seminary building for earthquake reinforcement and the structural remodeling of the south wing as a residence for our senior members began in 1990. Christened Casa Claret, the south wing was dedicated in May 1992, providing appropriate housing for senior members of the community, some of them still engaged in reduced forms of ministry.

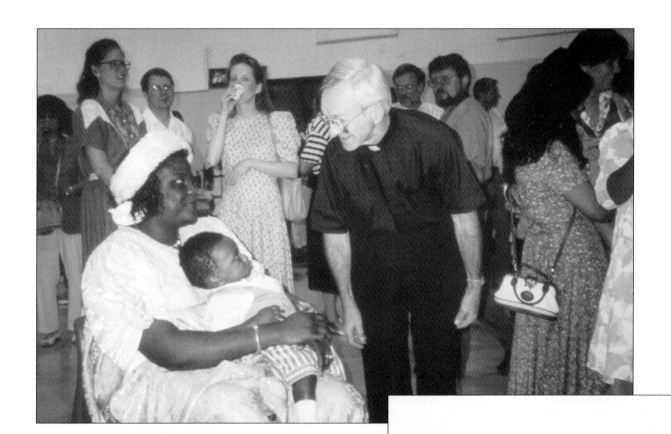

Corpus Christi Parish, Stone Mountain, Georgia, 1992

After much discussion and debate, the Eastern Province Ad-Hoc Committee on English-speaking ministries presented their resolutions regarding a new ministry to the Claretian Mini-Assembly gathered at Glenview, IL. The proposal to accept pastoral leadership at Corpus Christi Church was overwhelmingly approved. At the time, the parish was the fifth-largest in the Archdiocese of Atlanta with 2,745 registered families from a variety of ethnic and racial groups.

Fr. Luis Olivares and the Sanctuary Movement, 1990

During the 1980s the political turmoil in Central America forced many families to enter the United States for safety and security. The Catholic Church became one of the leading organizations offering sanctuary to these refugees. Under the pastoral leadership of Fr. Luis Olivares at Our Lady Queen of Angels Church (La Placita), the parish declared itself as a sanctuary for affected immigrants. Its Centro Pastoral Rutilo Grande offered tutoring classes, counseling, special liturgies, and the formation of Christian Base Communities for the residents. This commitment to immigrant rights continues to this day.

Immaculate Heart of Mary Seminary, St. Anthony Claret Seminary, San Antonio, Texas, 1994–1995

The new student residences in San Antonio provided the Claretians an opportunity to undertake theological studies at the Oblate School of Theology. Initially housed in the original Claretian foundation house, a new residence was later established on the city's West Side.

Center for Prayer, Annunciation House, Long Beach, California, 1999

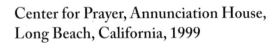

In celebration of the 150th anniversary of the Claretian Missionaries, the Western Province began a new ministry in Long Beach. Known as the Center for Prayer, the storefront ministry provided a refuge for an urban area plagued by drugs, prostitution, and violence. Different programs were offered to meet the needs of the local residents.

Annunciation House became the residence for the Claretians connected to the ministry and complemented the evangelical witness sponsored at the Center for Prayer.

Nuestra Señora de la Esperanza, Cuidad Juárez, Chihuahua, Mexico, 1999

The Ciudad Juárez mission commemorated the 150th anniversary of the establishment of the Claretian Congregation by creating a joint ministry on the United States/Mexican border. The U.S. Eastern and Western Provinces and the Mexican Province collaborated to serve a new community, Tierra Nueva, a factory town created to manufacture goods for export. With a community of 50,000 residents, the Claretians staffed the main church, Nuestra Señora de la Esperanza, and three outlying *capillas*.

Jamaica Mission, Kingston, Jamaica, 2001

Faithful to its commitment to serve the global church, the Eastern Province accepted the invitation of Archbishop Edgerton Clarke of Kingston to serve at Our Lady of the Angels Church in the capital city. Formerly a Franciscan priory, the church had no resident priest for five years. To assist the archbishop, the congregation also ministered at the neighboring church, St. John the Baptist Parish. The Claretians accepted the challenge to reinvigorate both parishes and reengage the laity in the life of the local church. Pictured is Fr. Thomas McGann, Pastor.

Tepeyac House, Los Angeles, California, 2005

This house was originally founded as a vocation discernment community in February 2005. The purpose of the house changed in August 2008, becoming a Novitiate House. Currently it serves as an apostolic house of hospitality for all who need a temporary base in Los Angeles. This includes Claretian international visitors.

Los Angeles Assembly, Loyola Marymount University, Los Angeles, California, 2009

The process to discern the unification of the United States Provinces began at a week-long meeting at Loyola Marymount University. A series of speakers and ample time for socialization allowed the Claretians from both Provinces to meet each other, share their hopes and concerns, and make plans for the future.

Claretian Missionaries – United States of America Province, Techny, Illinois, 2012

The Claretian Missionaries – USA Province was formally ratified with the election of Reverend Rosendo Urrabazo as provincial. The new province included all Claretian ministries located within the geographical boundaries of the nation.

Blessing and Rededication of the Foundation House, San Antonio, Texas, 2013

One of the first symbolic acts of the new Province was the two-year restoration of the original foundation house in San Antonio. The first Claretian-owned property in the United States was restored to its original specifications. The house served not only Claretians ministering at San Fernando Cathedral, Immaculate Heart of Mary Church, and other Texas missions but also welcomed Mexican religious refugees who sought sanctuary during the Mexican Cristero revolt. This house now serves as the main residence for Claretians ministering in San Antonio.

Acknowledgments

Many people contributed their time and talents to make *The Claretians in America: A Pictorial History 1902–2012*, a reality.

Special thanks is given to Patricia Lawton and Jency Liddell of the Catholic Research Resources Alliance and Jean McManus of the Hesburgh Library at the University of Notre Dame, who went beyond the call of duty to provide newspaper scans for the book. The short-lived mission in Dodge City, Kansas, proved to be difficult to document, but with the help of Timothy Wenzl, Archivist of the Diocese of Dodge City, and Denise Eggers of the Paulist Library in Washington, DC, we were able to find an image of the Mexican railroad worker community in 1915. Maria Mazzenga, Education Archivist at Catholic University of America, provided the means whereby we could professionally digitize an image from the Paulist publication *Missionary News* from May 1915.

The Archdiocese of Los Angeles Archival Center provided information about the Claretian arrival in California. We are appreciative that Associate Archivist Jim Beardsley handled our request promptly. Likewise Meg Hall of the Archdiocese of Chicago's Cardinal Joseph Bernadin Archives and Records Center was helpful in sharing the letter that launched Claretian ministry in the Upper Midwest. We also appreciated Lisa Gonzalez's assistance in locating a photograph of the original building at the Catholic Theological Union. Joshua Zimmerman of the Archives of the Archdiocese of Seattle shared photographs of the Claretian ministry in Washington State. Alma Nieto of La Purísima Church in Orange, CA, proved to be a God-send as we needed a photograph of the church where the Claretians served for many years. Finally, William Maxwell of the Bank of Stockton Photographic Collection gave us permission to reprint a photograph of St. George's Church, which was an elusive item!

Brother Edward Loch of the Archives of the Archdiocese of San Antonio, Eric Hartmann of the Catholic Archives of Texas in Austin, and Carlos Cortez of the University of Texas at San Antonio Special Collections have been helpful in sharing advice and photographs for this work.

Special thanks to those who made this book possible and the Claretians who patiently proofread and critiqued the work so that it reflects the rich and varied history of the United States Province's expression of St. Anthony Mary Claret's vision.

Photo Credits

The majority of the photographs come from the Claretian Missionaries Archives USA Canada located in Chicago, IL.

Courtesy of Catholic Archives of Texas, Austin, p. 2.

093-0008 (Main Plaza and San Fernando Cathedral ca.1902), General Photograph Collection, MS 362, University of Texas at San Antonio Libraries Special Collections, San Antonio, Texas, p. 4.

Missionary News (May 1915), Paulist Library, Washington, DC, p. 17.

Archdiocese of Chicago's Cardinal Joseph Bernadin Archives and Record Center, IL, p. 25.

Cabriniana Collection, Cabrini College Library, Radnor, PA, p. 25.

Warren School of Aeronautics, CA, p. 32.

Smit Young Photography, Chicago, IL, p. 40.

Catholic New World, Chicago, IL, p. 42.

Urbanowicz Photography, Chicago, IL, p. 43.

Beacon Photography, Chicago, IL, p. 48.

Mueller Photography, Chicago, IL, p. 49.

Lake County Discovery Museum, Curteich Postcard Archive, Wauconda, IL, pp. 50, 120.

Casteñada Photography, Los Angeles, CA, p. 61.

Ricci Studio, CA, p. 63.

Mika Studio, NJ, p. 64.

Weaver Studio, Los Angeles, CA, p. 71.

Christy Sheperd Photography, CA, pp. 77-78.

Courtesy of Bank of Stockton Photographic Collection, CA, p. 81.

Ed Lettau, pp. 84-85, 87, 98, 101, 114, 125.

Reni Newsphotos, Inc., DC, p. 89, 93.

John Wright Photographer, CA, p. 92.

Pontrelli Studios, CA, p. 100.

Dominguez Adobe at Rancho San Pedro © 1984 United States Postal Service. All Rights Reserved. Used with Permission., p. 105.

Courtesy Archives of the Archdiocese of Seattle, p. 113.

Catholic Theological Union, Chicago, IL, p. 119.

John Rodriguez, pp. 120, 132, 143.

La Purísima Church, Orange, CA, p. 126

Antonio Perez, IL, pp.128, 133, 135, 139.